A Study Guide to…

C000133094

Blood Brothers for GCSE

All Tiers

By Janet Marsh

INTRODUCTION

The material contained in this pack is meant to supplement and enhance learning at Key Stages 3 or 4. The exercises and worksheets will enable teachers of English to offer practice in reading, writing, speaking and listening skills. In addition, there will be opportunities to access background information where appropriate to enhance understanding and appreciation of texts.

Every effort is made to ensure that the information provided in this publication is accurate. It is the policy of Coleridge Press to obtain permission on any copyright material in their publications. The publishers will be glad to make suitable arrangements with any copyright holders whom it has not been possible to contact.

Purchasers may photocopy the sheets in this pack provided that they do so only for use within their own institution.

ISBN 978-0-957493-54-4

Text by: Janet Marsh
Design and Layout by: David Jones

Published by Coleridge Press

Copyright © Coleridge Press 2013

Act One

The Prologue

After the overture has finished, Mrs Johnstone comes forward and sings:

'Tell me it's not true
Say it's just a story.'

The Narrator tells the audience what the ending of the play will be; twins born not knowing their relationship and dying on the same day. The Narrator's words are in verse, rhyming, unlike the dialogue of the rest of the play, setting it apart.

The function of a prologue in literature is multi-purpose. A prologue is a short introductory piece included at the beginning of a novel, play or poem. It can be as short as a poem with a few lines or as long as a full-length chapter. It can serve several purposes, including giving background information, establishing the tone and setting, hooking the reader into the story, and introducing characters and conflicts:-

- One function of a prologue is to provide background information for the reader. It can introduce incidents in the past that are important to the current story. Historical happenings that are critical to the plot and characters in the story can be highlighted, although they also may be given more description later.

- Another function of a prologue is to establish the tone and setting of the story. The setting also can be introduced, because where and when a story takes place also can be essential to how the plot and conflicts play out or are resolved.

- For novels and plays, another function of a prologue is to hook readers into the story. The small part they read in the prologue may have just enough information or interesting situations that they will want to read further. Especially when prologues are short and provide only brief information, they serve to heighten the interest of readers quickly so they will want to continue reading.

- Prologues also exist to introduce characters and conflicts. They can go ahead and let the reader see inside the actual story and learn what has happened and what may happen in the future by letting them in on the action and the characters.

One of the most famous prologues appears in Shakespeare's **Romeo & Juliet** at the beginning of the play. Visit the following link where an actor explains the function of the prologue:-

http://www.bbc.co.uk/learningzone/clips/romeo-and-juliet-prologue/9892.html

NOW THINK ABOUT
Which of these functions do you think the Prologue serves in this play?
Do you think that the play is spoiled by having the end revealed to the audience?

The Bargain

We see the Narrator taking on the part of the Milkman who is demanding money from Mrs Johnstone. She tries putting him off but he is wise to her excuses. She tells him she's starting a new job and will be able to pay him. We hear the voices of her children off stage all telling her they're hungry and she tells them that once she is earning, they'll be able to have anything to eat they want and then they'll '*go dancing.*'

We see her now at work, pregnant, cleaning for Mrs Lyons in the smart part of town. Mr Lyons is away on business a lot and clearly Mrs Lyons is lonely. They bought a big house for the children they never had. She obviously regrets this and Mrs Johnstone is struck by the fact that she can't seem to stop having children and Mrs Lyons can't have them. At that point Mrs Lyons puts a pair of new shoes on the table and Mrs Johnstone is horrified, saying it means bad luck. Though she denies she's superstitious, she tells Mrs Lyons that you should never put new shoes on the table.

Superstition

Look at the following list of superstitions concerning bad luck.,

Superstitions can be defined as "irrational beliefs, especially with regard to the unknown" (Collins English Dictionary).

<u>Bad Luck</u>

Unlucky to walk underneath a **ladder**.

Seven years bad luck to **break a mirror**. The superstition is supposed to have originated in ancient times, when mirrors were considered to be tools of the gods.

Unlucky to **see one magpie**, lucky to see two, etc...

Unlucky to **spill salt**. If you do, you must throw it over your shoulder to counteract the bad luck.

Unlucky to **open an umbrella in doors**.

The **number thirteen** is unlucky. Friday the thirteenth is a very unlucky day. Friday is considered to be an unlucky day because Jesus was crucified on a Friday.

Unlucky to put **new shoes on the table**.

Unlucky to **pass someone on the stairs**.

The Twins Are Parted

The Narrator steps in to remind us about other superstitions concerning bad luck, then turns himself into a gynaecologist examining the pregnant Mrs Johnstone. He tells her she's expecting twins. Mrs Johnstone is horrified by this; times are hard for her as it is, and with two extra mouths to feed, she can't imagine how she is going to cope. She's afraid that she might lose her children as she's already had the Welfare snooping around. She tells Mrs Lyons she **'loves the bones'** of all of them but children need more than just love to live on. It is at this point that Mrs Lyons suggests that she gives her one of the twins. Her husband is away, she can stick a cushion up her jumper to look pregnant and no one need ever know.

She gives some compelling reasons to Mrs Johnstone as to why this arrangement will work well;

- Mrs Johnstone has too many children already
- Mrs Lyons has none
- If Mrs Johnstone cannot cope with the children she has, Social Services might take them into care
- She'll be able to see the child every day
- The child would have the best of everything as the Johnstones are well off

She does her utmost to persuade Mrs Johnstone who really does sympathise with her longing for a child. In a song sung by the two women, Mrs Johnstone imagines what a great life the child would have; **'a bike with both wheels on,'** **'you'd never find him effin' and blindin.'** There is a moment of real emotion when the two women embrace and Mrs Lyons tells Mrs Johnstone she must help her and the bargain must be sealed properly. She makes Mrs Johnstone swear on the Bible -a dramatic moment which is registered by the Narrator: **'In the name of Jesus, the thing was done.'**

 This dramatic moment is merged with the birth of Mrs Johnstone's babies whom she wheels home, only to be met by all those she owes money to - the Catalogue Man, the Finance Man. She tells the audience how difficult it has been for her to resist buying things she can't afford:

'When y'look in the catalogue an' there's six months to pay, it seems years away.'

 Faced with having her things repossessed, Mrs Johnstone is philosophical: she tells the Catalogue man that the table was repossessed one night as they were sitting and eating their tea! We see other creditors taking goods from her house as she stands and sings **Easy Terms.**

The words of the song take on a poignancy as she sings to the babies in the pram; the idea of returning things you can't pay for *'living on the never never'* mean far more then acquiring goods on hire purchase. Mrs Johnstone knows she must give up one of the twins and that there will be a price that she'll have to pay eventually.

NOW THINK ABOUT

Where do your sympathies lie at this point in the play? Can it ever be right to give up a child for economic reasons? Or to allow someone else the benefit of becoming a parent?

In the past, women didn't always have the choice of whether to give up their babies as this extract from a newspaper article shows.

- Controversial Government programme ran between the 1950s and 1980s
- Mothers often had their newborns taken before they had even held them
- They were pressured, deceived and threatened to give up their children
- Some were shackled to beds and drugged before signing consent forms

Surrogacy

ITV's Coronation Street has been running a plot line based on surrogacy.

Surrogacy is an arrangement in which a woman carries and delivers a child for another couple or person. The surrogate may be the child's genetic mother (called traditional surrogacy), or she may be genetically unrelated to the child. In a traditional surrogacy, the child may be conceived via home artificial insemination using fresh or frozen sperm or impregnated via IUI (intrauterine insemination), or ICI (intracervical insemination) performed at a health clinic

The most frequent reason for this practice is female infertility or in some cases, the female is fertile but for health reasons cannot risk pregnancy

Money can change hands in this process, as in the case of the *Coronation Street* plotline............

· CORONATION ST. ·

'Coronation Street' surrogacy plot ending revealed

Published Friday, Jun 21 2013, 09:42 BST
By Sophie Dainty
46 comments

133	56	21
👍Like	🐦 Tweet	🇶 +1

Tina with baby 'Joe'

Coronation Street's surrogacy plot will finally come to a conclusion over the coming weeks.

Tina McIntyre will eventually decide to do the right thing and hand over baby Jake to his biological parents.

© ITV

Viewers will know that Izzy (Cherylee Houston) and Gary (Mikey North) were left devastated when Tina (Michelle Keegan) decided she couldn't part with the baby she has renamed Joe.

However, when a heartbroken Izzy announces that she is calling off the fight for 'Joe', Tina is suddenly plagued with doubts over whether she is doing the right thing.

After being hit by the realisation that what she is doing is wrong, Tina eventually agrees to give up her rights to the baby and hand him over to his parents.

Izzy's dad Owen throws a party to celebrate and gives a speech in the Rovers in which he thanks Tina for everything she has done.

 The plotline explored the complex feelings that both women especially experienced when it was time to give up the baby. The resolution of the plotline was reminiscent of a much older story, from the Bible where King Solomon was asked to settle a dispute between two women, each of whom claimed a baby was hers by right.

That is a story from the Bible about King Solomon and his wisdom. (1 Kings 3:16-28). The story is about two women who both give birth around the same time. One night one of the mothers rolls over and kills her baby by accident. Then she switches babies and pretends that it was the other mother's fault. The next morning the mothers fight over the baby and the problem is presented to the King. He suggests that they cut the baby in half so each mother can have a part of him (the baby). Then one woman cries out and says that the other woman can have the baby. King Solomon then concludes that the woman who would give up the baby to save its life is the real mother and the baby is given to her.

Mrs Lyons reminds Mrs Johnstone of their promise and she demands one of the twins. She doesn't want to give the baby up and begs for a bit more time with him, but Mr Lyons is due home and the deed must be done. Reluctantly, with words of **Easy Terms** repeated in her song, Mrs Johnstone agrees, returning home without the baby who he tells the other children has died.

Mrs Johnstone is Fired

Now that Mr Lyons is home and the baby is settled in, Mrs Lyons is nervous that the secret will be revealed by Mrs Johnstone who is always fussing around baby Edward. When she is alone with her husband, Mrs Lyons says she thinks Mrs Johnstone should be sacked and as he's a busy man and the house is her responsibility, he tells her to do what she thinks best. When the women are alone, Mrs Lyons says she is dissatisfied with Mrs Johnstone's work and gives her fifty pounds as a leaving settlement. But Mrs Johnstone is not so easily bought off; if she has to go, she says, she will take her son with her, but Mrs Lyons says if she tells the police what has happened, she will be prosecuted. In desperation she makes up a superstition that if twins are secretly parted and one learns the truth, both twins will die. The superstitious Mrs Johnstone is speechless at this and Mrs Lyons seizes her advantage and pushes the money at her as if to complete the bargain.

At this point the Narrator sings **Shoes upon the Table** which mentions several superstitions, linking them with the devil and symbols of religion like a rosary. The words of the song are menacing as they speak of the devil *'staring,' 'creeping'* and echo Mrs Johnstone's fears about what she has done and that this will have serious consequences in the future.

People in Western contemporary cultures recognise saying, "God bless you" when someone sneezes as a polite response. The seemingly simple blessing has deep roots running through the Elizabethan Era as when an Elizabethan told a sneezing person, "God bless you," she was performing a spiritual protection. Elizabethans believed when a person opened his mouth to sneeze, the devil could use that as an opening to enter into the person and possess her. Saying "God bless you" protected the sneezer from demonic possession.

Even now there are superstitions that feature the devil.

Blood Brothers

 The play now moves on seven years. We meet Mickey who is playing with a toy gun, **foreshadowing** the way both twins will die. He has been playing near the big houses near the park though his mother has warned him to stay away from them (this is where the Lyons family live). Mickey doesn't want to do as he is told and recites a poem in which he imagines what fun it would be to be his brother Sammy who's nearly ten and can do all kind of daring things and get away with them - swimming, drawing nude women, weeing through letter boxes, spitting, and going to bed late. As he sits and thinks about all these things he envies, Edward appears and the boys start talking to each other. Immediately it is obvious that, although they are twins, their upbringing has been totally different.

Already we see the importance of upbringing or nurture in the play.

 Many studies have been carried out about whether our genetic makeup determines how we develop or whether the way we are brought up - where we live, where we are educated, the values our parents give us, how much money our family has - makes us into what we become.

If twins are brought up in a totally different way, will their genetic similarities be enough to establish a bond?

Twins

Much research has been done into the behaviour of twins. The Internet article that follows tells us of some of the research findings.

Gemellology is the term for the scientific study of twins. These multiples possess a very special and unique bond. Most twins hold more than simply good friendship, rather, they begin to bond as life - long companions beginning before they are even introduced to the world. In most cases, <u>identical twins</u> share a stronger bond than that of

fraternal twins, primarily due to the fact that they share the same genes. Obviously, twins are very similar simply by sight, but it is unimaginable the extent to which twins are identical in their thought patterns, pathological, psychological, and physical aspects.

Many identical twins experience the same thought patterns because of their shared genes. Ron and Roger Scarbrough scored so similarly on a test that their teacher failed them, convinced they were cheating. Given another chance, they again made the same errors. When joining the air force, they had to take a test, and mysteriously answered the same questions wrong. When retested, they again made the same one error.

Janie and Linda N. are identical twin sisters. Their thought patterns were proved to be very similar when they both sent their parents the same exact present thousands of miles apart from each other. Twins reared apart at birth and later brought back together reveal further proof of the similar thought patterns of identical twins. Dr. Thomas J. Bouchard's studies at the University of Minnesota states that he has met twins who both store rubber bands on their wrists, sneeze in public for attention, and pairs who walk into the ocean backward.

NOW TRY THIS

Using the internet to research, find five to ten of the most interesting facts you can about twins. Are you able to see any shared similarities yet between Mickey and Edward? If so, what are they?

The following article looks at a real life case of separated twins.

Twins Reunited

Mary and Elaine are identical twins... but they didn't get to meet each other until they were 30 years old - despite living only a few miles apart in Derbyshire.

The pair, who grew up in Chesterfield, are identical twins who were separated at birth. They lived apart for three decades.

And yet each of them somehow had a feeling they were not totally unique in the world. At the age of five, Mary says she "discovered the existence of another me."

Mary and Elaine were born at the end of World War II to the unmarried 19-year-old Leah Cohen. She had been disowned by her family and was living in a Leeds boarding house. One twin was adopted by Paddy and Lavinia Logan but they were not rich enough to take on both.

Lavinia adopted Elaine while Mary went to another family on the understanding that there would be no contact between them. The girls were sent to different schools to make sure they didn't meet.

But destiny had other plans for the girls.

At the age of five, Elaine was walking in town with her mother when she saw a poster showing a group of local children with the actress Patricia Dainton

Twins: Elaine Logan and Mary Holmes

"I was certain one of them was me," recalls Mary. But of course it wasn't - it was her sister. Three years later, Mary was playing in the waiting room of her doctor's surgery when another child joined in. But Mary's playmate kept calling her Elaine - and Mary didn't know why. Soon after, Mary's adoptive mother, Doris Black, realised she had to come clean about what had happened and told her she had a twin sister.

Elaine, on the other hand, was completely aware of the fact that she had a sister as her less strict parents had been open with her as soon as she was able to understand.

Mary aged 19

But still, they weren't allowed to meet.

The twins continued to make their own way in life - Mary went to live in Singapore, Elaine in Surrey. The two had tried to make contact - but fate was working against them at that time.

Eventually, Mary and her husband moved to Scotland. Mary knew by now that Elaine had been adopted by a family called Logan, that one of the Logans was called Vincent and that one of the family was a professional dancer.

One evening, Mary was watching The Tom Jones Show on TV which featured a group of dancers known as The Young Generation. At the end of the show, the credits rolled - and Mary watched as the name Vince Logan scrolled up. She recalls: "It kind of jumped out at me from

the screen... I was sure it was Elaine's brother's name. I wrote to him care of the BBC... just in case it was him. And it was!"

Elaine at 22

So from then, the twins were in touch. But still, distances, pregnancies and illnesses kept the pair apart. Letters and phone calls were exchanged regularly - but it was another two years before they could actually meet.

"Straight away there was a bond," remembers Elaine. "The minute we started talking it was like we'd known each other all our lives. We just chatted like we were the greatest friends ever."

"All you can say it that it was like looking into a mirror. It felt very strange, very odd."

Elaine and Mary in America, 1984

Now, Mary and Elaine have been together longer than they have been apart. Together, they have taken part in twins research in America which in itself helped cement their relationship as it was the first time they had the chance to spend time alone - something the twins had missed out on in their formative years.

NOW THINK ABOUT

What similarities have you found between Mary and Elaine's story and Mickey and Edward's? Give examples for the play so far.

Mickey and Edward get on so well that when they find out they were born on the same day, they agree to be blood brothers. The arrival of Sammy with his talk of guns strikes a different note. He doesn't think much of Edward, calling him *'a friggin poshy'* but Edward is too busy looking at his head to see if he can see the 'plate' that Mickey says he has inside it!

Mrs Johnstone appears and Mickey introduces his 'brother', Edward Lyons, whom he has given the name of Eddie - though no one else calls him that. Mrs Johnstone is shocked to see her son and tells him to go and not come back - or the bogeyman will get him. As he leaves she sings *Easy Terms* which now has nothing to do with money or debts but with the agony of losing her son.

At Home with the Lyons Family

Edward returns home where his father has bought him a toy gun, yet another visual reminder of the ending of the play. Mr Lyons is obviously busy at work. His wife tells him she wants him to spend more time with Edward, to be a major part of his life.

Edward is looking up bogeyman in his dictionary but his mother tells him *'It's superstition. The sort of thing a silly mother might say to her children.'* At that moment Mickey rings the bell to ask if Eddie is coming out to play. Mrs Lyons knows that this is Edward's twin and gets rid of him, making Edward angry and resulting in him calling her *'a fuckoff.'* Horrified, she hits him hard and tells him she doesn't want him growing up *'with boys like that,'* then realises she has been very harsh and cuddles him to her with words of love.

Games

Children are in the street playing cops and robbers, cowboys and Indians. Edward, forbidden now to play with Mickey, stands watching the games. Linda and Mickey are in one gang, Sammy in another. As usual Sammy is doing the shooting but all the children know that in these games, no one is ever hurt and:

'You can get up off the ground again

It doesn't matter

The whole thing's just a game.'

All the games merge from one into the other as the children play games inspired by TV (like *The Untouchables*), cowboy films and war films. Sammy appears as a mad professor with a condom filled with water which he pretends is a bomb.

Mickey

The rules of the games are simple; if you cross your fingers when you are shot / blown up, it doesn't count. The children, led by Sammy, turn on Mickey but he's got Linda to support him. She accuses Sammy of stealing from her mother and he backs down, taking his gang with him. Mickey is suddenly struck by a fear of dying though Linda tells him that at least if he dies and goes to heaven, he'll be with his twin again.

Mickey's dark mood passes and he's pleased to have taken Sammy's air pistol which he intends to show Edward. They call on Edward and though he's not supposed to, he goes out to play with them.

Linda

Edward is excited by their bravado- they do things he would never do like cheeking a policeman and altogether, playing with them is much more exciting than his own life where he seems to be wrapped in cotton wool.

The Narrator sets the mood for the scene that follows here with his song 'There's Gypsies in the Wood' with its powerful line 'they're going to take your baby away'.

Eddie

Seeing Edward spending time with Mickey and disobeying her makes Mrs Lyons very nervous. We see her in a scene with her husband where she shows how anxious she is. Her husband of course cannot understand why as he is unaware of the bond between the boys. He tells her she should see a doctor 'for her nerves' and shouldn't be bringing him home from work about every small concern about Edward. She insists they should move and that she is 'frightened' for Edward but of course she can't explain why. Without thinking he picks up a pair of Edward's shoes from the floor and puts them on the table as they are talking, causing his wife to sweep the shoes off; she seems to be infected by Mrs Johnstone's superstition as the Narrator sings 'the devil's got your number'.

The Policeman

The scene shifts to the park where the three are playing with Sammy's air pistol, though they get bored with this and consider throwing stones through windows. As they prepare to do this, a policeman sneaks up behind them and asks them what they are doing. Edward gives his name as Adolf Hitler, but realises Linda and Mickey had only been bragging earlier about their dealings with the police. The three children, now in tears, are bundled off home by the policeman.

We then see Mrs Johnstone being told off by the policeman. He has had occasion to speak to her before about Sammy. He warns her that if she doesn't keep Mickey under control, *'it'll be the courts for you.'*

When we see him call at the Lyons' house, the policeman behaves quite differently.

1.   Look at the following sections of the text which deal with the policeman's visit.

<u>Mrs Johnstone</u>

Policeman: *And he was about to commit a serious crime love. Now do you understand that? You don't wanna end up in court again, do y'? Well that's what's gonna happen if I have any more trouble from one of yours. I warned you last time, didn't I? Mrs Johnstone, about your Sammy?*

Well there'll be no more bloody warnings from now on. Either you keep them in order, Missis, or it'll be the courts for you or worse, won't it?

<u>Mr and Mrs Lyons</u>
The policeman had removed his helmet and holds a glass of scotch.

Policeman: *An'er, as I say, it was more of a prank really, Mr Lyons. I'd just dock his pocket money if I was you (laughs). But, one thing I would say, if y' don't mind me sayin', is well, I'm not sure I'd let him mix with the likes of them in the future. Make sure he keeps with his own kind, Mr Lyons. Well, thanks for the drink sir. All the best now. He's a good lad, aren't you, Adolph? Goodnight sir.*

My Friend

Edward has been told by his parents that they are moving to the country and  he goes to Mrs Johnstone to say goodbye and tell her he doesn't want to go. She gives him a picture of Mickey / his twin and herself in a locket as a keepsake. There is a touching moment between Edward and Mrs Johnstone where a bond is established. Edward gives Mickey a toy gun as a leaving gift. We see the Lyons family in their new country setting but the birds Mrs Lyons is so delighted by are recognised by Edward as magpies (*one for sorrow, two for joy*....) Mr Lyons comforts his wife by telling her that it'll be a while before they are fully settled.

Meanwhile, Mickey is missing Edward. Sunday afternoons seem to be the worst time for him when he is lonely, bored and aimless. He sings *Long Sunday Afternoon* and from his new house in the country, Edward sings *My Friend*. Both twins show from the words of the song how much they long for the companionship of their twin and how much they appreciate the differences between themselves and their 'friend.'

Mickey speaks of Eddie: *'Wearing clean clothes, talking properly, like doing sums and history like.'*

While Eddie obviously respects Mickey who can: *'kick a ball and climb a tree like.'*

In the next part of the scene, Mrs Johnstone has received a letter from the council rehousing her in the country. This episode which ends Act One tells us a lot about how the Johnstone family have been living and how the community sees them.

Mrs Johnstone's excitement and relief are infectious and the audience are pleased for her and the family, even though Sammy is trying to ride on a bull. The act ends on a humorous note and in an upbeat way so that we almost forget what the eventual outcome of the play will be.

Questions on Act One

<u>Try these as written questions to test your understanding of Act 1</u>

1.   Do you have sympathy in the play so far for Mrs Johnstone? Do you agree that *'there's a stone in place of her heart'*? Give your reasons fully and remember to give examples to back up what you say.

2.   What disadvantages does Mickey have in his upbringing, compared with Edward? Give examples and refer to the text.

3.   Imagine that you are Donna Marie Johnstone. Write a letter telling a friend about the news that the family is moving to the country. You could include:-

     a. general family news - is Sammy in trouble again?

     b. your feelings about the move - remember you've always lived in the city so you'll miss your friends.

     c. what your mother's reaction has been.

     d. attitudes of the neighbours.

4.   Write about the kind of life Mrs. Johnstone and her family live, using evidence from the first act of the play.
     Organise your answer into paragraphs about:-
     • her marriage and pregnancies
     • the way she speaks
     • where and how she lives
     • her attitude to life.

Act Two

Moving to the Country

Mrs Johnstone's life has taken a turn for the better; the neighbours do fight a little *'but never in the week.'* Instead of being persecuted by the Milkman, he takes her dancing and she calls him Joe. He's even sympathetic to Sammy's spot of bother – he burned the school down but was given probation. Even the judge was sympathetic when he saw Mrs Johnstone who reminds him of Marilyn Monroe - though she draws the line at going dancing with him.

Now the twins are fourteen and Mickey is conscious of his appearance and girls. The rest of the children have now flown the nest, Donna Marie keeping family tradition alive by having three children already. From her song it's clear that Mrs Johnstone often thinks of *'that other child of mine'* and hopes he is well.

The scene then changes to The Lyons's house where Mrs Lyons is teaching Edward to dance. He is away at an all boys public school and says he rarely gets to see any girls, let alone dance with them. When he leaves he asks her what she means when she says that they are *'safe.'*

The scene shifts to Mickey and Mrs Johnstone who is trying to get him off to school. Linda is waiting for him at the bus stop and Sammy is on his way to the dole. As all three get on the bus, Mrs Johnstone is smiling happily now that her life seems to have come together at last. However, the conductor changes into the Narrator who reminds her that *'no-one can embark without the price being paid.'*

The mood darkens further when Sammy is refused a child's ticket and holds up the conductor at knife point. He runs away and Linda tells Mickey that he had better not follow his brother into crime or else she won't love him. Mickey is embarrassed by this but Linda simply doesn't care:
'I don't care who knows. I just love you. I love you!'
In Edward's school, there is talk of Edward going to Oxbridge.

Education

The following information is adapted from the Internet. Read it then think about why Mickey is unsuitable for Oxbridge and Edward is suitable. Use information you have gathered from the play so far.

Oxford University

Properly speaking, there's nothing to distinguish Oxbridge (a made-up combination of **Ox**ford and Cam**bridge**) from the rest of England's university system. Oxford and Cambridge are just two of the many fine universities to be found around the country. And yet in some ways these two are unlike any other.

As the two oldest universities in England with eight hundred years of history and among the most well known in the world, they have come to be seen by some as representing the very finest traditions of scholarship, while others see them as examples of wealth and privilege that would never let in 'ordinary' student.

The play takes place before the comprehensive system of education that most of us are familiar with. Mickey attends a <u>secondary modern school,</u> *'all boredom and futility'* - Russell says in the stage directions.

We see Mickey in class at his secondary modern school with Linda. The lesson seems to be a particularly pointless one – about the diet of the Boro Indians who live in the Amazon basin. The teacher bullies Mickey who is bored and can see no point in what he is being taught. Linda stands up for him and Mickey replies to the teacher, making a joke out of the whole lesson and his attitude. In the end the teacher suspends both Mickey and Linda and the word 'suspend' is picked up immediately in the next sequence on stage where Mrs Lyons receives news of Edward's suspension.

In order to appreciate the vast differences there were in education at 11 for pupils in seventies Britain, you could read the following articles which will help you understand the different world of

Cambridge Dictionaries Online
The most popular online dictionary and thesaurus for learners of English

comprehensive (school)
noun [C] UK 🔊 UK

Definition

▶ a school in the UK for children above the age of eleven of all abilities:
the local comprehensive
a comprehensive education

Mickey and Edward and how these would have such an impact on their lives.

A **secondary modern school** is a type of secondary school that existed in most of the United Kingdom from 1944 until the early 1970s and was designed for the majority of pupils - those who do not achieve scores in the top 25% of the eleven plus examination. They were replaced in most of Britain by the comprehensive school.

The 1944 Butler Education Act created a system in which children were tested and streamed at the age of eleven. Those who were thought unsuitable for either an academic curriculum or a technical one, were to be sent to the secondary modern, where they would receive training in simple, practical skills. Education here was to focus on training in basic subjects such as arithmetic, mechanical skills such as woodworking and domestic skills, such as cookery. In an age before the advent of the national curriculum, the specific subjects taught were chosen by the individual school.

The secondary modern came to be seen as the school for failures. Those who had 'failed' their eleven plus were sent there to learn rudimentary skills before advancing to menial jobs. Secondary moderns prepared their students for the CSE examination, rather than the more prestigious O level, and although training for the latter was established in later years, less than one in ten children took advantage of it. Secondary moderns did not offer schooling for the A level, and in 1963 only 318 former secondary modern pupils sat A levels. None went on to university.

Secondary moderns were generally deprived of resources and good teachers. Staff turnover was high and continuity in teaching minimal. Not all secondary moderns were as bad, but they did generally suffer from neglect by the authorities.

The poor performance of the 'submerged three quarters' of British schoolchildren led to calls for reform. Experiments with comprehensive schools began in the 1950s, hoping to provide an education which would offer greater opportunities for those who did not enter grammar schools. By 1976, with the exception of a few regions secondary modern schools had been formally phased out.

For the top quarter of Britain's eleven year olds, the grammar school beckoned. These schools taught an academic syllabus, their pupils wore uniform and they were considered traditional and high achieving schools which attracted the best teachers. Many had long histories of education in Latin and Greek. To be accepted into grammar schools, you had to pass the 11+ or as it was sometimes called 'the scholarship'.

11+

Take a look at the following eleven plus style of question. Remember you would sit it at <u>eleven,</u> not the age you are now!

In these questions, the same letter must fit into both sets of brackets, to complete the word in front of the brackets and to start the word after the brackets.

4. THI ( ) ECK   STU ( ) OON

B ^C   D ^C   N ^C   K ^C

5. FOR ( ) ILL   PAC ( ) ICK

N ^C   H ^C   M ^C   K ^C

6. SHE ( ) ONE   COR ( ) INE

N ^C   D ^C   L ^C   S ^C

Answers
4=D   5=K   6=D

Read the following comprehension and answer the questions.

The Stranger

The man in the dark overcoat looked rather strange to the children. Sam and his sister, Eloise were staying at a holiday cottage on the Welsh island of Anglesey for their summer holiday. Their parents, Steve and Jackie Turner had taken them to the nearby town of Bangor for the day. They had visited the Cathedral and were looking around the shops when they came across the stranger in the dark overcoat, standing in the doorway of an empty shop. He had a peaked cap over his black hair and he seemed to be in pain.

"I wonder what he's doing, standing there?" enquired Sam in a quiet voice, so that the man would not hear.

"I don't know," replied his sister. "He doesn't look particularly friendly."
"Hurry up!" shouted their father, a few feet further on. "It looks like it's going to rain soon."

With that the Turner family went into a local cafe for a cup of tea and some cakes, just as it started to rain. A few minutes later as they were pouring out their tea, Eloise saw the stranger go past. He was walking with a definite limp and his face seemed to be looking towards the ground.

"Eloise!" shouted her mother. "Your tea's getting cold."

"Sorry mum," replied Eloise, her mind wrapped up in thoughts about the stranger.

By the time the family had finished their tea and cakes, it had stopped raining. Large puddles of rainwater were everywhere. They were making their way back to the car park when they heard a commotion ahead.

A few metres ahead they could see the stranger being held by two policemen. He was struggling and shouting something out in a language they couldn't understand. Several people were looking at what was going on. He was being put into a police van just as the Turners arrived at the car park.

"I wonder what all that was about?" remarked Dad as he opened the car. "No doubt it'll be in the local newspaper tomorrow," replied Mum.

Questions

1. What was the name of the island on which the Turner family were staying?

_____

2. What building in Bangor had the family already visited that day?

_____

3. Apart from the overcoat, what was The Stranger wearing?

_____

4. Where did the family go after seeing the stranger?
a) the cathedral **b)** the park **c)** a cafe **d)** the police station

_____

5. What part of speech is "definite" (line 15)?

_____

6. What does the word "commotion" mean (line 22)?
a) movement **b)** anger **c)** jumping **d)** disturbance

_____

7. What is the literary term for "struggling and shouting something?"

_____

8. Whereabouts were the Turner family when all this was happening?

_____

9. What finally happened to The Stranger?

_____

10. Write in your own words who you think The Stranger was.

_____

Answers

1. The island was called Anglesey.
2. The family had already visited the Cathedral in Bangor that day.
3. The passage tells us that he was wearing a peaked cap.
4. **c)** A cafe.
5. "Definite" is an adjective.
6. The word "commotion" means disturbance.
7. The literary term for this is alliteration.
8. The Turner family was making their way back to the car park.
9. He was put in a police van OR the stranger was arrested.
10. Any sensible and imaginative answer - e.g. I think that the stranger was an escaped prisoner.

NOW THINK ABOUT

Do you think comprehensive schools are a better / fairer way to educate children after the age of eleven?

Of course Edward is at a FEE PAYING school which you could argue gives him even greater privileges. Schools where parents have to pay to send their children are fee paying and some of the most famous and PRESTIGIOUS (*distinguished, famous*) are called PUBLIC SCHOOLS – though they are not intended for most people.

It's ironic that at this point of the play, both Mickey and Edward are suspended from their very different schools. What are the reasons for their suspension?

Biological Parents

When Mrs Lyons sees the locket, she is horrified that her past has come back to haunt her. When she demands that Edward tells her his secret, she says to him:

'But I'm your mother.'

> **NOW THINK ABOUT**
>
> **Do you think of Mrs Lyons as Edward's mother? Or Mrs Johnstone?**

Mickey seems unwilling to return Linda's affection and she gets very fed up with him and tries to make him jealous by mentioning a good looking boy she's seen. It's obvious that Mickey does care for her but he lacks self confidence and is all too aware of how he looks. He knows he doesn't have the smoothness and ease of someone like Edward and he doesn't know what to say.

Using the internet to research, find five to ten of the most interesting facts you can about twins.

Both boys sing **That Guy** *separately, admiring what they think*

the other has which makes him special, then they realise who the other is. Edward is very impressed by Linda and the fact that she is Mickey's girlfriend, though Mickey admits they he doesn't have the words to tell her how she feels. Edward knows exactly what to say and suggests that they could both further their education about women by going to see *Nymphomaniac Nights* and *Swedish Au Pairs*.

When Mickey pops home to get some money, Mrs Lyons, who has seen them together, follows them.

Once again the persistent song of the Narrator remind us that *'the devil he's still got your number'* and there will be no avoiding the tragic outcome.

The boys go to Mrs Johnstone's house and although they try to cover up what they are going to see in the cinema, Mrs Johnstone knows full well it's pornography and tells them they are **'randy little sods,'** though she is more amused than shocked.

Mrs Lyons calls at The Johnstone house and confronts Mrs Johnstone, admitting that she has never felt that Edward is truly hers. She says:

'I took him. But I never made him mine.'

She offers Mrs Johnstone thousands of pounds to move away and when she is refused, in desperation she grabs a knife from the drawer and goes for Mrs Johnstone, cursing her and calling her a witch. No damage is done, but we hear the children's chorus with its refrain of **'High upon a hill there's a woman gone mad.'**

The boys have come out of the cinema dazzled by the naked flesh they have seen. They bump into Linda and her friend who have also seen the adult films. Everyone is in good humour and Edward climbs up a lamppost where he is spotted by a policeman but the others give him the slip and the scene segues into a typical summer scene at the funfair where the three are shooting at the rifle range which becomes a game of piggy-in-the-middle, Linda being in the middle, which signifies how both boys want her as their girlfriend. The song points us to them all growing up in their teens, spending time together, being happy when life is still uncomplicated., taking snaps of each other, having a trip to the seaside. However, the words take on a deeper significance as the story brings us up to the boys at eighteen.

All this is conveyed on the stage by mime from the three main characters and the words of the Narrator, always ready to point the tragedy ahead:

'An' you don't even notice broken bottles in the sand

The oil in the water.'

We now arrive at the point when Edward is ready to leave for university. He and Linda meet up in the street and he asks her if he can write to her.

Although she loves Mickey, he has still not asked her to be his girlfriend and Edward tells her that if he were in Mickey's shoes, he would not hesitate to tell her he loved her.

Mickey then joins them, having worked late at the factory, doing a job he hates. The last thing Edward does before he leaves is to push Mickey into asking Linda to go out with him as his girlfriend.

Life goes on for Linda and Mickey while Edward's away at university and Linda gets pregnant. Mrs Johnstone agrees to let them live with her and is disappointed that things have not turned out better for them. Sadly she says to Mickey:

'You've not had much of a life with me, have you?'

Marriage

The scene shifts to Mickey and Linda's wedding.

In the seventies when the play is set, there was a greater tendency for babies to be born inside wedlock. Often when a single woman found she was expecting a baby, the wedding would be rushed forward to make sure the baby was born after the wedding. This was known colloquially as a *shotgun wedding* - the idea being that the woman's father holds a shotgun to the head of the man who has made her pregnant, forcing him to marry her – or else!

Attitudes to marriage and pregnancy have changed almost beyond all recognition since the seventies.

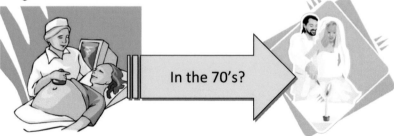

In the 70's?

This newspaper article comments on the way attitudes to marriage have changed over the past decades.

The proportion of children born to unmarried mothers hit a record 46 per cent last year, the Office for National Statistics said in its annual update of births in England and Wales.

This was up from 45 per cent in 2008, 25 per cent in 1988 and just 11 per cent in 1979.

The figures have alarmed some family experts, who have warned that children were more likely to suffer from poverty and poorer educational achievements if they came from unmarried parents.

Others, however, pointed out that some of the trend was down to middle class couples choosing to have a child before going on to get married.

The figures confirmed the revolution that has happened to family life over the last generation. Babies born out of wedlock, considered shameful in many circles as recently as 25 years ago, are now almost in the majority.

Having a baby now comes before marriage as the key milestone in many women's lives. The average age of a woman getting married is now 33.8 years, while the average age of giving birth is 29.4 years, the ONS said.

While the figures showed a steady decrease in the number of "sole registrant" births, when there is no name of the father on the birth certificate – as occurred on the birth certificate of Ed Miliband's son Daniel – it did show a substantial increase in the number of births outside of marriage.

In 2009, 326,069 of the total 706,711 births were outside of marriage.

Anastasia de Wall, director at Civitas, the think tank, said that the figures were not necessarily a cause for pessimism, pointing out that cost of weddings put many couples off from tying the knot. "Some of this is down to a reordering of priorities for many people, especially the middle classes.

"You make your commitments in order of importance. So that can mean getting a mortgage together, than having your first child and only then getting married. For many an expensive wedding is less important than living together and bringing up a child together."

The average cost of a wedding, a recent survey suggested, had climbed by £5,000 in the last five years to reach more than £20,000.

Recession

We see the wedding which rapidly becomes Mickey's sacking as Mr Lyons, the symbol of the employer sings of such redundancies being *'a sign of the times'*.

In the seventies there was a recession which stemmed from the sudden rise in oil prices worldwide. This resulted in job losses and the failing of many businesses. At present Britain is in the grip of another recession which some argue is even more serious.

Read the following which tells us more about the background in which *Blood Brothers* was written.

Britain has now endured eight recessions since the Second World War. The early ones in the late 1950s and early 1960s were both short - lived and relatively shallow.

Then, in the early to mid - 1970s, an oil price shock helped cause larger contractions in output and a surge in inflation – so called "stagflation." If there is any decade over the past fifty years we'd rather forget, then this would be it.

High unemployment and the infamous winter of discontent ensured that voters turned against the then Labour Government in the hope that things would improve. The **"Winter of Discontent"** is a term used to describe the British winter of 1978 – 1979, during which there were widespread strikes by local authority trade unions demanding larger pay rises for their members.

Public sector employee strike actions included an unofficial strike by gravediggers working in Liverpool and Tameside, and strikes by refuse collectors. Streets were piled high with rubbish. Additionally, NHS ancillary workers formed picket lines to blockade hospital entrances with the result that many hospitals were reduced to taking emergency patients only.

The election posters for the Conservatives declared *Labour isn't Working*, a reference to the 1.4 million out of work.

Whilst the strikes were largely over by February 1979, the government's inability to contain the strikes earlier helped lead to Margaret Thatcher's Conservative victory in the 1979 general election and legislation to restrict unions.

As Miss Jones joins the dole queue the Doleites sing that in time she'll get used to unemployment and regard it as *'leisure'* and just *'another sign of the times.'*

With Mickey on the dole, Christmas approaches and Edward returns from university, totally unaware of how life has changed for his friends. When Mickey explains what life is like living on the dole and giving no hope in his life, Edward takes it all very lightly, seeing it as an amusing *'bohemian'* life. He tells Mickey he would:

'tilt my hat at the world.'

But the realistic Mickey reminds him that he doesn't:

'Wear a hat I could tilt at the world.'

When Edward offers money, Mickey refuses and calls the blood brothers bond that Edward reminds him of *'kids' stuff'* and tells his friend that:

'While no one was looking I grew up.'

He explains that he doesn't blame Edward but their worlds are so different he doesn't want to see him.

Prison and Death

Edward bumps into Linda who he obviously still likes a lot. She tells him she's pregnant and that she and Mickey got married two weeks before. Sammy offers Mickey money to take Linda out, fifty pounds, to be lookout for a robbery he is planning; there will be guns, he says, but only for the look of it.

We then see the hold-up at the petrol station which goes wrong. Sammy shoots a man and in the confusion, Mickey is arrested and given seven years in prison where depression overcomes him and he is prescribed anti-depressants:

Sammy

'just like Marilyn Monroe' as the Narrator tells us, to stop his mind from *dancing*.

He becomes addicted to them inside and when he gets out, both Linda and his mother are worried about his addiction. They both want him to get his life back on track - a job, someone to live - but Linda has it all in hand. She says she has got them somewhere to live:

'it was some feller I know. He's on the housin' committee.'

When we see Linda and Mickey together he is very agitated looking for his pills. He cannot do without them, he says, though he has tried. He makes it clear he knows where the help has come from - the house, the job. Councillor Eddie Lyons has arranged it all and Mickey understandably feels helpless to look after his wife and family. He tries to explain to Linda that he takes them *'to be invisible.'*

Linda is at the end of her tether and rings Edward and the Narrator comments on the difficulty of Linda's life, married too young, a husband in prison, living with her mother-in-law. Mrs Johnstone joins in with her comments too, brushing aside Linda and Edward's affair as *'a light romance…nothing cruel.'* We see Edward and Linda meeting, kissing and then Mickey at work, trying very hard to come off the pills. The tension builds, underlined by Mrs Johnstone's song and comes to a climax when Mickey gets the gun Sammy hid years before. We see Mickey searching the town, followed by his mother. The Narrator's speech builds the tension even further with its repetition of the words *'mad man'* and the refrain *'the devil's got your number.'*

Mrs Johnstone calls on Linda to warn her about Mickey and they rush towards the Town Hall where Edward is in a meeting and addressing members of the council.

Mickey has appeared holding the gun with two hands to steady it. He confronts Edward and accuses him of taking everything away from him. He has given up the pills for her sake but now he has lost her. He tells Edward that it was Mrs Lyons who revealed the affair to him. He is so incensed he even questions whether his daughter is really his and not Edward's.

The police arrive and try to get Mickey to put down the gun. Mrs Johnstone has got into the council chamber and tells Mickey that Edward is his brother. Mickey is filled with rage and screams out:

'Why didn't you give me away! I could have been him.'

Mickey shoots his brother and the police shoot him.

It is up to the Narrator to sum things up and point the moral which is what the Chorus did in traditional Greek tragedy:

'And do we blame superstition for what came to pass.

Or could it be what we, the English, have come to know as class.'

Mrs Johnstone sings the song *Tell me it's not True* which weaves together the themes of the play - only a game, Marilyn Monroe, two people (twins). The cast picks up the song with its ideas of illusion, pretence, an old film that isn't true.

Themes

Class

Mrs Johnstone

Think about the evidence in the play that firmly places Mrs Johnstone in the working class.

Think about:-

- her job
- her education
- how she speaks
- how / where she lives.

Money

The importance of money in the play is bound up with issues of class. Where the Johnstones and the Lyonses live  is determined by how much money they have, which is in turn determined by the work they do - which in turn will probably be determined by how they did at school. If our lives are dictated by our financial circumstances, then money is the key.

Mrs Johnstone does not have enough money - not just for treats and toys for the children but to feed and clothe them, though they get by. She cannot pay the milkman and begs for extra time to do so, but his answer is simple:

'no money, no milk'.

She fantasises about all the things she'll be able to buy when she starts her new cleaning job:
'Roast Beef, Yorkshire Pudding, Battenberg Cake
When I bring home the dough.'

The harsh reality of her life is that:
'kids can't live on love alone.'

Mrs Johnstone gives up Eddie because her finances are so carefully balanced that she could just about cope with one child, but two will tip the balance. She also wants a better life for him. Once the deal is struck, it becomes a *'debt that must be paid,'* even though at this point no money has changed hands.

Even before Eddie is handed over, Mrs Johnstone is reminded by her many creditors that:

'Y' shouldn't sign for the bloody stuff if y' know y' can't pay.'

But Mrs Johnstone is only human, and an optimistic one at that. The lure of credit and HP is just too strong to resist, especially when repayment seems *'years away.'*

Her song *Easy Terms* is full of deeper meaning with its references to:
'The price I have to pay' as she links giving away Eddie with:
'living on the never never.'

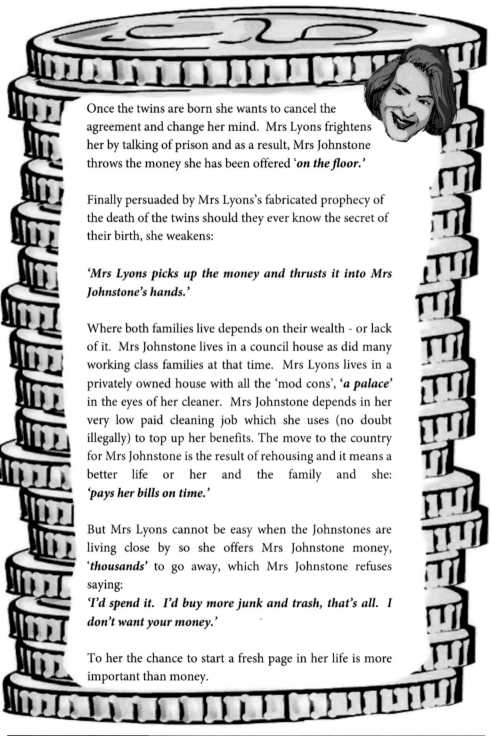

Once the twins are born she wants to cancel the agreement and change her mind. Mrs Lyons frightens her by talking of prison and as a result, Mrs Johnstone throws the money she has been offered *'on the floor.'*

Finally persuaded by Mrs Lyons's fabricated prophecy of the death of the twins should they ever know the secret of their birth, she weakens:

'Mrs Lyons picks up the money and thrusts it into Mrs Johnstone's hands.'

Where both families live depends on their wealth - or lack of it. Mrs Johnstone lives in a council house as did many working class families at that time. Mrs Lyons lives in a privately owned house with all the 'mod cons', *'a palace'* in the eyes of her cleaner. Mrs Johnstone depends in her very low paid cleaning job which she uses (no doubt illegally) to top up her benefits. The move to the country for Mrs Johnstone is the result of rehousing and it means a better life or her and the family and she: *'pays her bills on time.'*

But Mrs Lyons cannot be easy when the Johnstones are living close by so she offers Mrs Johnstone money, *'thousands'* to go away, which Mrs Johnstone refuses saying:
'I'd spend it. I'd buy more junk and trash, that's all. I don't want your money.'

To her the chance to start a fresh page in her life is more important than money.

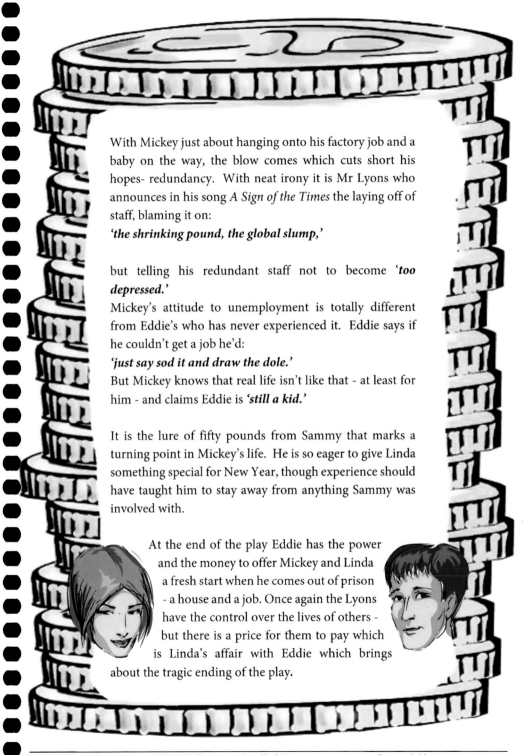

With Mickey just about hanging onto his factory job and a baby on the way, the blow comes which cuts short his hopes- redundancy. With neat irony it is Mr Lyons who announces in his song *A Sign of the Times* the laying off of staff, blaming it on:

'the shrinking pound, the global slump,'

but telling his redundant staff not to become **'too depressed.'**

Mickey's attitude to unemployment is totally different from Eddie's who has never experienced it. Eddie says if he couldn't get a job he'd:

'just say sod it and draw the dole.'

But Mickey knows that real life isn't like that - at least for him - and claims Eddie is **'still a kid.'**

It is the lure of fifty pounds from Sammy that marks a turning point in Mickey's life. He is so eager to give Linda something special for New Year, though experience should have taught him to stay away from anything Sammy was involved with.

At the end of the play Eddie has the power and the money to offer Mickey and Linda a fresh start when he comes out of prison - a house and a job. Once again the Lyons have the control over the lives of others - but there is a price for them to pay which is Linda's affair with Eddie which brings about the tragic ending of the play.

The article that follows outlines some of the social and economic background of the play. This will give you some background to one of the most important social issues of the play.

HOUSING IN BRITAIN

At the end of the First World War the then prime minister, David Lloyd George, had a vision of 'Homes for heroes', houses built by local councils to replace the poor slum conditions that existed for the working classes. These were the first 'council houses' but it wasn't until after the Second World War that a huge house building programme began where one million houses were built, 80% of them council houses, to replace those destroyed by Hitler.

The house building boom continued when the Conservatives returned to power in 1951, but the emphasis shifted at the end of the decade towards slum clearance, as millions were uprooted from cramped, rundown inner-city terraces and rehoused in purpose-built new towns or high rise blocks.

A generation was introduced to the joys of indoor toilets, front and rear gardens, and landscaped housing estates where, as the town planners boasted, a tree could be seen from every window.

But the post-war dream of urban renewal quickly turned sour.

By the early 1970s, the concrete walkways and "streets in the sky" that had once seemed so desirable were becoming grim havens of decay and lawlessness.

It was against this backdrop that "right to buy" began to take off, with the number of council houses sold in England going up from 7,000 in 1970 to nearly 46,000 in 1972. Tenants were offered the right to buy their houses at a fraction of the market value, giving ordinary working class families the opportunity to improve their properties, sell for a profit and leave them to their families.

The Labour Party bitterly opposed the "right to buy", arguing that it would lead to a dangerous reduction in council housing stock. This was exactly what happened. No new investment in building what we term "social housing" was made and many people who would

have been council tenants twenty years before were forced into substandard and expensive private housing, leaving the council houses as the last resort for problem families and those on benefits.

Today there are calls for a renewed building programme of social housing, especially since the recession and the collapse of the banking system have made getting on the housing ladder beyond the reach of many people.

Being rehoused in the country with:

'a new situation

a new destination' is not an option now as it was for Mrs Johnstone.

FOR DISCUSSION

Having a decent place to live and bring up any family you may have will be a major factor in your life. Where do you want to live? What sort of housing will it be? Will it be near family and friends? How much is it likely to cost?

How will you pay for it? Will it be rented accommodation? Will you hope to buy somewhere to live? Do you hope to have Housing Association support? Would you expect to have support from the government if the costs are too high for you to afford?

DIVIDE INTO GROUPS AND DISCUSS THESE ISSUES THEN CHOOSE ONE SPOKESPERSON TO REPORT BACK WITH A SUMMARY OF WHAT YOUR GROUP'S THOUGHTS WERE.

Women

Although Russell's play is called **Blood Brothers**, the fate of the twins is linked to their mothers, birth and surrogate. Women, whether mothers, girlfriends, wives or even Hollywood legends, are at the core of this play and their influence is felt throughout.

The most crucial roles for women in the play are those of birth and surrogate mothers. Mrs Johnstone is embarrassingly fertile:

'havin' babies is like clockwork'

she tells Mrs Lyons who having got her big house is still waiting to conceive. She tells the pregnant Mrs Johnstone:

'we thought children would come along'

but Fate has decided otherwise. Infertility however is not to be simply accepted and Mrs Lyons hopes to adopt, believing:

'an adopted child can become one's own'

and this will form the basic plot of the play.

What kind of mothers do the women prove to be? Mrs Johnstone is warm, funny but chaotic. Even before the twins are born, she cannot feed and clothe her children properly and spends her life dodging the rent man, the milk man and the catalogue man .A chorus of children shows us the kind of conditions they live in:

'I'm starvin' and there's nothin' in.'

It is easy to be judgmental about her parenting skills but she has been abandoned by her husband and is trying every way she can to earn enough to support her family. However, she has little control over Sammy's illegal and antisocial activities and she turns a blind eye to bad language, truancy and pornographic films. At the end of the play we know that Donna Marie has followed in her footsteps and has three children already.

On the other hand, Mrs Lyons has been more involved with Eddie's upbringing but she doesn't have to work, has only one child and a husband with a good job. Eddie at seven speaks well, has good manners, is obedient – at least at first - he recognises rules and boundaries and in effect Mrs Lyons is the 'better' mother. But her secret makes her over protective and paranoid because deep down she does not feel that Eddie is her child, revealing that:

'I took him but I never made him mine.'

Whatever the difficulties of bringing up their children, Russell shows us two women who would do anything for them. When Mickey is forced into a shotgun wedding with Linda, Mrs Johnstone, seeing history repeating itself, says sadly:

'You've not had much of a life with me, have y'?'

Another of the roles that women take on in the play is that of girlfriend/lover/wife, a role that all three women have played at some time in their lives. Mrs Johnstone had been **lovelier than Marilyn Monroe** when she married but a succession of pregnancies had aged her until Mr Johnstone went off, leaving her pregnant with the twins. Even a few years later she is still attractive to Joe the milkman and even the Judge offers to take her dancing! When she sees Eddie and Linda later in the play attracted to each other, even

though Linda is married to Mickey, she still sings of a *light romance, nothing cruel*, showing herself to be a romantic still and aware of the importance of love among the daily grinding routine of life:

'the girl within the woman

who's waiting to get free

she's washed a million dishes

and she's always making tea.'

Mr and Mrs Lyons seem to have a conventional marriage; he works hard, talks of *merger*s and *board meetings* and is annoyed when she calls him home from the office. Though he wants a baby, he doesn't show much interest in Eddie as he is growing up. Their house is big, Mrs Lyons doesn't work, can afford a cleaner and waits to become pregnant. Her adoption of Eddie throws her whole well ordered life into paranoia and anxiety as she is terrified that the secret will be discovered. Eddie achieves at school, goes on to university, enters local government but the problems of her position as adoptive mother overshadow the rest of her life and her marriage seems unfulfilled.

Linda has loved Eddie ever since their neighbourhood games together. She dries his tears when he says he doesn't want to die, she defends him in the classroom against the teacher's sarcasm, she wants him to stay away from Sammy, she tells him she loves him at fourteen but it takes him until he is eighteen for him to ask her to be his girlfriend. When she is pregnant, marriage is taken for granted and she lives with Mrs Johnstone and Mickey. The romance in Linda's life is provided by Eddie whose song before he goes off to university says:

'if I was him I'd bring you flowers and ask you to dance.'

When Eddie is able to help with housing and Mickey has been acting like a zombie while taking the tranquilizers, Linda is almost inevitably drawn to Eddie, even though:

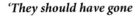

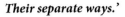

'They should have gone

Their separate ways.'

This betrayal tips Mickey over the edge and the awful irony is that it is Mrs Lyons who informs Mickey. As he tells Eddie,   Linda represents the only thing he has left in his life and now his 'friend' has taken that:

'How come you got everything an' I got nothing?'

Set against the lives of ordinary Liverpudlian women is one of the most poignant motifs of the play, Marilyn Monroe, the glamorous Hollywood star whose life at first glance seems a world away.   In references throughout the play, she is the young and glamorous Mrs Johnstone, and her replacement who tempts Mr Johnstone away from his responsibilities.   But she also represents the darker side of life when in jail Mickey:

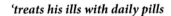

'treats his ills with daily pills

Just like Marilyn Monroe.'

The Marilyn motif is even used in the play to create a sense of the passing of time. At the end, the action of the play is compared with;

'an old movie of Marilyn Monroe.'

In her own troubled life, the icon of glamour and sexuality did not find lasting happiness as a daughter, wife, lover or mother, though more ordinary women might find fulfillment in all or at least some of those roles.

Childhood

Russell does not glamorize childhood in the play. It is not an idyllic time sheltered from the harsh realities of adulthood. Even Eddie, growing up with a doting mother in a comfortable environment becomes stifled by secrets and paranoia, making him want to break out into a more adventurous and spontaneous childhood where you can push boundaries, take risks and have fun.

If Mrs Johnstone has:

'seven hungry mouths to feed

and one more nearly due.'

it's little surprise that so far life has been no picnic for her children who early on complain of being hungry and not being able to sleep.

To Mrs Johnstone cleaning her employer's grand house, it would be wonderful to offer a child this *'palace...*

...with a garden to play in and his own bed, he'd never get into trouble.'

When Mrs Johnstone tells the children that the *'other twinny'* has died, they all imagine him in heaven riding his own *'bike with both wheels on'* and this leads them all to list the things they would like to have in their lives, items beyond Mrs Johnstone's means, even with the help of the catalogue.

But however little they have, the children still have the imagination and the spirit to play games, street games like Mounties and Indians, gangsters. Mickey can hardly wait until he gets to play more grown up games like Sammy does-building underground dens, weeing through letterboxes and drawing *'nudey women.'* And of course playing with guns,

The Johnstone children are left to run wild with few checks on their behaviour and language; Eddie does not have the same freedom. He tells Mickey;

'my mummy doesn't allow me to play down here actually.'

When he hears the forbidden words that Mickey utters so casually, he's excited as children are. Both he and Mickey are mystified by the plate in Sammy's head, taking the expression literally which are what children do. It can't be a dinner plate, they agree, so if it's smaller, it must be a tea plate!

In childhood whatever the game - gangsters, cowboys, soldiers - the whole thing's *'just a game'* and you can get out of it, stay alive just by crossing your fingers, and this idea echoing through the play gives it poignancy, especially in the final moments.

For Eddie however childhood isn't a time for running wild. His mother says:

'I don't want him out playing'

and when her husband accuses her of being over protective, she says his new friends are:

'drawing him away from me.'

Eddie's childhood is a lonely bookish existence where he behaves like a small adult. No wonder he is excited by the prospect of throwing stones, cheeking policemen and uttering forbidden words. He tells Mrs Johnstone he'd:

'much rather live here.'

When he has had Mickey to play with and the tie of their birth is so strong that both boys are bored when left completely to their own devices in *Long Sunday Afternoon,* you see the boys as two parts of a perfect whole.

Eddie doesn't have the need for friends after he has moved to the country because his parents send him off to boarding school which must have suited Mrs Lyons very well because he is now out of the way of any further meetings with his blood brother. Clearly they have the money to pay for this type of education and feel it offers their son a good start in life. It also protects him from the kind of educational experience which is offered Mickey and Linda - pointless information thrown at them by a bored and sadistic teacher. One of the clever ironies of the play is the fact that each blood brother is suspended from two very different schools for very different reasons - the forbidden locket and backchat in the classroom. With Eddie set for university and Mickey for a dead end job, their fates are sealed, a grim thought for all those who cannot escape the laws of nature and nurture.

Rags to Riches

But not everything that happens to you in life can be put down to your upbringing.

Take a look at these mini-biographies of three famous people.

Her Cash Will Go On - Celine Dion

Celine Dion is still ranked as one of the highest-grossing female entertainers and in 2007 was listed as the fifth richest female entertainer, coming in at $250 million. She also was ranked as the top-earning singer of the decade by U.K.'s *The Sun.* Not bad for the 14th (!) of 14 children growing up in a poor household in rural Quebec, where her father made $160 per week to support the family of 16.

Like many of these rag-to-riches stories, it seems Celine's success owed as much to luck as talent - she was discovered singing when she was 12 and continued to create more songs and make more money.

Making it with Music - Jay-Z

Another music mogul that made his way from the bottom to the top is Shawn "Jay-Z" Carter. Carter began his life in the Brooklyn's Marcy Housing Projects. Carter was raised by his mother, and was involved in crime when growing up - at 12 he shot his brother in the arm for stealing his jewellery.

Carter began as a rapper and went on to become involved in everything from nightclubs and clothing to being a part owner of the New Jersey Nets. As of 2009, Carter was worth over $150 million.

The Phenomenon - Oprah Winfrey

Surely the most well-known rags-to-riches story of our era is the story of Oprah Winfrey. Having been born into abject poverty in rural Mississippi, Winfrey went from being a young girl clothed in potato sacks (literally) to the richest and most powerful female media mogul in the world. Winfrey was able to accomplish this by moving from a disruptive and abusive household in with her stricter father.

Once Winfrey was subject to discipline and was supported at school, she became an honours student and got her big break when she became a newscaster in Nashville after finishing college. Winfrey has come a long way from her poor upbringings, and is worth $2.9 billion.

Superstition

There are numerous references to superstition in the play:-

➢ new shoes on the table
➢ a joker in the park
➢ spilled salt
➢ a lone magpie
➢ the promise made upon the Bible
➢ the made - up superstition that if one of a pair of twins parted at birth finds out, they will both die
➢ killing a spider
➢ breaking a mirror
➢ walking on pavement cracks
➢ the devil's got your number
➢ crossing your fingers
➢ gypsies in the wood
➢ never look at one magpie
➢ if the mad woman catches your eye you will never grow any further
➢ the bogeyman
➢ the black cat stalking
➢ your number's up

These are woven into the words of some of the characters - notice how Mrs Lyons picks up Mrs Johnstone's superstition when she sweeps the shoes off the table in the scene with her husband - but most references to superstition come from the Narrator.

Motifs

In a narrative, such as a novel or a film, **motifs** are recurring structures, contrasts, or literary devices that can help to develop the piece's major themes. The narrative motif is the vehicle by means of which the narrative theme is conveyed. The motif can be an idea, an object, a place or a statement. In *Of Mice and Men* the motif of the vulnerable animal like the mouse and the puppy that Lennie kills is a way of foreshadowing the end of the novel and a reminder of the violence in animal / human behaviour.

In *Blood Brothers* the motif of guns, dancing and Marilyn Monroe are significant.

Guns

Willy Russell said that he didn't think that banning toy guns would curb aggression in children.

There are numerous references to guns in the play which foreshadow the ending:

KIDS: Why can't I have an air pistol?
MICKEY: (aiming the gun at her and firing)
MICKEY: Mam, our Sammy's robbed me other gun.
(Edward's father produces a toy gun for him. Edward ceases it and shoots his father,
SAMMY: I'm gonna get a real gun soon.
SAMMY: I got y' / I shot y'
LINDA: Look…we've got Sammy's air gun.
SAMMY: We don't use the shooters.
SAMMY: Listen, it's not a toy.
MICKEY: You shot him, you shot him.
SAMMY: (Pulls up a floorboard and puts the gun beneath it).
NARRATOR: He's gonna shoot somebody down.
MICKEY: (A gun held two handed to steady his shaking hands.
MRS JOHNSTON: Mickey don't shoot Eddie.

to guns, briefly describing where they appear.

Dancing

In most instances this is seen as a happy, uninhibited expression of joy:-

- Mrs Johnstone and her husband went dancing in their happier times and at their wedding. Though she felt like dancing when the children came, he wouldn't go with her - but he did go dancing with the woman he left her for.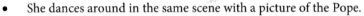
- When Mrs Johnstone is going to move, she hopes for a gentleman friend who might take her dancing.
- She dances around in the same scene with a picture of the Pope.
- Once she has moved and her life improved, she is taken dancing by Joe.
- The judge who sits on the case of Sammy who has burned down the school offers to take her dancing.
- As an adolescent, Mickey has started dancing.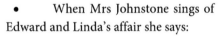
- Edward is given some dancing practice by Mrs Lyons.
- Edward begins to waltz Linda's mate around the street.
- Mickey promises Linda he will take her dancing and then have a slap up meal.
- On the tranquilisers Mickey's mind *'goes dancin'*.

- When Mrs Johnstone sings of Edward and Linda's affair she says:

'That same old tune

That always plays

And lets them dance as friends.'

Marilyn Monroe

Mrs Johnstone says of herself that when she was young she was:-

'sexier then Marilyn Monroe....'
'lovelier than Marilyn Monroe.'

When she starts having children she is

'twice the size of Marilyn Monroe.'

And he left her for a woman who:

'looked a bit like Marilyn Monroe.'

When she looks forward to her new job at Mrs Lyons's she thinks of the family as living like kings:

'like bright young things

like Marilyn Monroe.'

After the move to the country, Mrs Johnstone says that Joe said she had:

'legs like Marilyn Monroe.'

When Mickey is in jail and on tranquilisers, Mrs Johnstone compares him and his drug dependancy with Marilyn Monroe:

'and treats his ills with daily pills

just like Marilyn Monroe.'

The final words of the play remind us of *'an old film with Marilyn Monroe.'*

Tips for the Exam

The Extract

You may be asked to examine a piece of text in detail and answer questions on it. This question tests your ability to show you know not just what is going on in the extract which is a D grade skill, but also to examine the text **in detail,** referring to aspects of style in an analytical way. You will be expected to comment on the words spoken by the character (s) and on any STAGE DIRECTIONS shown.

Look at the following extract and the question that was set on it.

As in any close study of a text, it is essential to use the technique of:-

P   POINT   **E**   EVIDENCE   **E**   EXPLAIN

Take a look at this recent exam question.

Read the following extract carefully then answer the following question.

Look closely at how Mr and Mrs Lyons behave here. What does it reveal about their relationship?

Mrs Lyons: Oh, Richard, Richard.

Mr Lyons: For God's sake, Jennifer, I told you on the phone, he'll just be playing somewhere.

Mrs Lyons: But where?

Mr Lyons: Outside somewhere. With friends. Edward…

Mrs Lyons: But I don't want him out playing.

Mr Lyons: Jennifer he's not a baby. Edward…

Mrs Lyons: I don't care, I don't care.

Mr Lyons: For Christ's sake, you bring me home from work in the middle of the day, just to say you haven't seen him for an hour. Perhaps we should be talking about getting something for your nerves.

Mrs Lyons: There's nothing wrong with my nerves. It's just....just this place...I hate it Richard, I don't want to stay here anymore. I want to move.

Mr Lyons: Jennifer! How many times...The factory is here, my work is here.

Mrs Lyons: It doesn't have to be somewhere far away. But we have got to move, Richard. Because if we stay here, I feel that something terrible will happen, something bad.

Mr Lyons: Look, Jen. What is this thing you keep talking about getting away from? Mm?

Mrs Lyons: It's just.....it's these people...these people that Edward has started mixing with. Can't you see how he's drawn to them? They're...they're drawing him away from me.

Mr Lyons, in despair, turns away from her.

Mrs Lyons: Oh Christ.

He turns to look at her but she looks away. He sighs and absently bend to pick up a pair of children's shoes from the floor.

I really do think you should see a doctor.

Mrs Lyons: *(snapping)* I don't need to see a doctor. I just need to move away from this neighbourhood, because I'm frightened. I'm frightened for Edward.

Mr Lyons places the shoes on the table before turning to her.

Mrs Lyons: Frightened of what, woman?

Mrs Lyons: *(wheeling to face him)* Frightened of....... (*She is stopped by the sight of the shoes on the table. She rushes at the table and sweeps the shoes off.*)

What you have to do is put this small section of the text under the microscope, examining the following in detail:-

- Dialogue
- Stage directions

Do NOT summarise the extract; this is a low level skill and is not **analysis.**

Select from the text, by quoting, the most relevant words / phrases that you want to comment on.

NB. If you are not quoting from the extract **at all** when you are answering this question, you are not doing what is asked of you.

Look at the following answer to see how it's done.

The extract begins with Mrs Lyons fussing and panicking about Edward's whereabouts.

Mrs Lyons: Oh, Richard, Richard.

Mr Lyons: For God's sake, Jennifer.

We can see that she's agitated and stressed as opposed to her husband who seems calm but also annoyed at her overreaction. She is so stressed that she often cuts into what he is saying, interrupting him. In fact her speech is frequently unfinished, showing her agitated mood.

'It's just…just this place…'

Mrs Lyons seems more worried about other matters than his family.

'You bring me home from work in the middle of the day'.

He is clearly annoyed about being rung at work by his wife's seemingly trivial concerns. He is relaxed about Edward:

'Jennifer, he's not a baby' whereas his wife is over protective and cautious. Of course he doesn't understand her almost paranoid concern for Edward and he knows nothing of the secret - that Edward is not his son and was 'given' to his wife, one half of Mrs Johnstone's twins. This terrible secret has created a lie which will always be at the root of the Lyons's marriage.

When Mrs Lyons demands that they move away, her husband tells her is just not practical. We can see that she senses Edward might be in danger which foreshadows the ending, but although her husband tries to comfort her by 'putting his arms around her', he sighs, perhaps because he is irritated by her irrational behaviour or just calming her down so that he can get back to work. But when she persists, telling him they must move away, his frustration grows and he 'turns away from her', saying 'oh Christ' as if he can't take much more of her neurotic behaviour, his body language showing his lack of sympathy. He has already suggested that she sees a doctor 'for her nerves', repeating this as he picks up the pair of shoes, not realising the significance of putting them on the table.

His loss of sympathy with her is shown when he calls her 'woman' instead of 'Jennifer' or the more affectionate 'Jen' earlier in the extract.

When the suggestion is made, she 'snaps' and 'sweeps' the shoes off the table, showing that she has become as superstitious as Mrs Johnstone and that the immensity of what she has done and the secret she has to keep have driven her to the edge.

Overall this extract gives us the impression of a relationship on the verge of being destroyed by the terrible secret which has driven Mrs Lyons to fear and paranoia.

Now look at some more of the significant parts of the play and try the same approach:-

• The first meeting of Mickey and Edward.

What do we learn about characters of Edward and Mickey from their first meeting?

• The scene in the classroom where Mickey is suspended.

What do you see here of the relationship between Mickey and his teacher?

- The episode where Edward visits Mickey's house and says goodbye to Mrs Johnstone who gives him a locket.

What are your feelings about Edward and Mrs Johnstone in this extract?

Characters

These notes might be helpful for your revision on **Blood Brothers.**
In the text of play we only have:-
- stage directions
- the actual words spoken BY the character
- what they say ABOUT the character to form our opinions of that character.

When we see the play on stage, he DIRECTOR or PRODUCER will shape our views of the character by telling him/her HOW to play the scene /say the words / sing the song.

These notes sum up the main points about the characters in **Blood Brothers** USING THE TEXT AS EVIDENCE. Key quotes are in bold.

MRS JOHNSTONE

We're told by the Narrator:-
- **'there's a stone in place of her heart'**
- she's working class, speaks in a colloquial, Liverpudlian accent....
  'I'm back on me feet an' workin' the next day, y' know'
- she met her husband at a dance- shot gun wedding
- seven children at the age of forty two - used to look **'like Marilyn Monroe'**
- loves dancing

- now a single parent - always short of money

  'living on the never never'
- owes money all round rent – milk - catalogue
- works hard to support family, at poorly paid cleaner's job
- but won't accept **thousands** later on in the play from Mrs Lyons
- loves her kids - but can't control them
- superstitious - a Catholic (references to Rosary and the Pope)
- empathises with Mrs Lyons because she can't have children
- optimistic by nature - fresh starts

  'now that we're movin'

  'now that we're improvin'
- sense of humour (look at the words of her songs at the end of Act 1) - she can laugh at her situation
- can mimic the 'posh'
- amused by the adolescent Mickey and his attempt to look good
- amused by the trip to see the adult film- encourages the boys
- doesn't judge Mickey and Linda for her pregnancy- not a hypocrite
- knows she hasn't been much of a mother to Mickey
- worried about Mickey when he comes out of hospital dependent on the pills- supportive of Linda
- doesn't take the relationship of Linda and Edward too seriously - turns a blind eye

  'nothing cruel'

  'nothing wrong'

MRS LYONS

- pwns big house -had hoped for children- prepared to adopt but her husband is not. She says…

  'I believe that an adopted child can become one's own'
- speaks in Standard English, middle class - disapproves of bad language, rough children, will send Edward to public school, probably to become someone like his father
- quick witted - obviously more intelligent than Mrs Johnstone - resourceful- she comes up with the plan- thinks of all the details to make it real- manipulates Mrs Johnstone into accepting the deal (the oath)
- finds it easy to lie to her husband and Mrs Johnstone (the superstition about twins)

- heartless in her sacking of Mrs Johnstone and threatening that she will tell the police that she'd **'sold'** Edward
- anxious that her family is close- wants her husband to spend time with Edward
- she is terrified of Edward's contact with Mickey because of her secret and also because she wants to keep him cocooned from boys like that (she strikes him when he calls her a **'fuckoff)'**
- becomes paranoid about the friendship with Mickey, even picking up Mrs Johnstone's superstitious reaction to shoes on the table
- nervy, anxious, calling her husband home from work (he suggests she needs a doctor) saying she wants to move away
- she comes to realise

'I took him

But I never made him mine'

- Mrs Johnstone calls her **mad** after she goes for her with a knife and curses her Has her guilty secret made her so?
- in desperation, tells Mickey about Linda and Edward's affair, determined to do anything to break the bond of the blood brothers

MICKEY

- highspirited as the youngest, the butt of Sammy's bullying but keen to be just like him, doing all the forbidden things.
- intrigued by the plate in Sammy's head- loves swear words –his idea to be blood brothers
- tells Linda he's afraid of dying but cheered up that that would mean there's be no school
- boasts with Linda to Edward that he cheeks the police
- envies the ordered sort of life that Edward leads (My Best Friend) and when he's older (That Guy)
- as a teenager

'he's even started dancing, secret dancing'

- hates school – bored, disaffected
- insecure about girls- normal adolescent- Nymphomanic Nights
- tongue tied with Linda

'Erm...well, er, the thing is .... Linda, i've erm...Linda, for Christ's sake will you go out with me?'

- loves his mother

'You're great, you are Mam.'

- hated his job in the cardboard box factory but hates the dole even more

  'I'd crawl back to that job for half the pay and double the hours'
- has had to grow up quickly and has no sympathy with Edward's life

  'while no one was looking, I grew up'
- becomes a victim – takes the rap for Sammy- imprisoned- on tranquilisers

  'feelin' fifteen years older'

  'and his speech is rather slow'
- taking the tablets

  'to be invisible'
- at the end of the play, Mickey says to Edward

  'How come you got everything....and I got nothing?'
- And when he hears about the swapping of the babies he says to his mother

  (with almost uncontrollable rage)

  'I could have been him!'

EDWARD

- Obedient, well spoken, intelligent, middle class, polite, but excited by Mickey's daring

  'You know the most smashing things'
- Sammy calls him

  'a friggin' poshy'
- he shows affection to Mrs Johnstone when she gives him the locket

  'I think you're smashing'
- he envies Mickey as a teenager

  'If I was like him I'd know some real birds'
- But Edward knows how to speak to 'birds'- though all his knowledge comes from books
- He's more articulate than Mickey

  'I'd just tell you I love you'

  'if it was me'
- when he knows Linda is with Mickey he says he won't see her again but later when she goes to him for help, he cannot be so strong willed

The Essay

You will also be asked to write an essay on some aspect / aspects of the play. Questions for the Higher Tier usually ask you:-

- to examine a character
- to examine a theme / themes
- for your opinion on some issue of the play.

Some examples of these might be:-

1. Examine Russell's presentation of the Narrator in the play.
2. Discuss the way the theme of class is presented in the play.
3. For which character in the play do you have the most sympathy? Show how Willy Russell's presentation of your chosen character created sympathy for him / her.

These essays need planning. If you choose to answer on THEME, don't use the plot of the play as your plan e.g. "The play begins with Mrs Johnstone singing a song about Marilyn Monroe then.....". This will lead you into unnecessary story telling or _narrative_ which is going to mean your answer will not achieve more than a D grade. You may make some valid points in the course of it which will receive credit, but it will not show **focus** on the question. Use your answer book to plan your answer, using whichever method suits you best - spider diagram, bullet points etc.

Structure your answer by grouping your ideas together in paragraphs, remembering the:-

POINT   EVIDENCE   EVALUATION   technique.

Remember, these essay questions need a short introduction and a conclusion too. Try writing some sort of plan before you start - it will save time in the end and you will know where you're going. The overall **structure** will be better and this will be reflected in the mark.

Now consider this past question:

What do you think the Narrator adds to the audience's enjoyment and understanding of the play?

INTRO:	The part played by the Narrator is a little like the Chorus in a Greek play. He provides a commentary on the action making us think of the issues of the play, points us the moral at the end and pulls the play together, giving it a unity. As well as this, he takes on some of the minor roles in the play which help the action flow.
PARA 1:	prepares us for the end, reminds us of the sinister outcome - examples + quotes if possible.
PARA 2:	always associated with evil / superstition. Give examples - quote if you can.
PARA 3:	the milkman, the teacher at Edward's school. and Mickey's, the rifle range man, the photographer. How is the smooth action of the play helped by having these 'bit' parts played by him?
CONCLUSION:	plays a vital role, points us to the moral. And do we blame superstition or class?

Empathy Question

Popular questions on this text often ask you to **EMPATHISE** with characters

e.g.

> Imagine you are Mrs Lyons. At the end of the play you think back over what has happened. Write your thoughts and feelings. Remember how Mrs Lyons would speak when you write your answer.

Here you are being tested on:-

- What you know about Mrs Lyons's part in the play - what she did, what happened on stage, how she discovered about Linda and Edward's affair etc. in other words the PLOT.

- What kind of woman she is, what she felt about being able to have children, how she feared her secret would be discovered, how she was overprotective towards Edward, all of which should come through as you write your answer. You have to try to get 'under the skin' of the character to produce a good empathy answer and not simply say what went on. Remember, you will also write in FIRST PERSON **e.g.**